The race track and Sears, Roebuck and Co.'s
Building at the Illinois State Fair
at Springfield.

Greetings from ILLINOIS STATE FAIR Springfield Illinois

MACHINERY HALL AT STATE FAIR GROUNDS, SPRING...

No. 919. V. O. Hammon Pub. Co., Chicago

Arch & Dome Building, State Fair Grounds,
Springfield, Ill.

Illinois State Fair
1853   2002
150th ANNIVERSARY

Illinois State Fair

A 150 Year History

Photographs Courtesy of
Sangamon Valley Collection
Lincoln Library

By

Edward J. Russo, Melinda Garvert, and Curtis Mann

PUBLICATION STAFF

Authors: Edward Russo

          Melinda Garvert

          Curtis Mann

Photo Editor: Michael Bruner

Cover Design: Michael Bruner

Project Coordinator: Brad Baraks

Publisher: G. Bradley Publishing, Inc.

Commissioned by: Illinois Department of Agriculture

TABLE OF CONTENTS

Chaper 1: Wandering Fair 4

Chapter 2: A Home At Last 10

Chapter 3: A Changing Image......................30

Chapter 4: Fair Today, Fair Tomorrow 49

Acknowledgments 64

Please check the G. Bradley Publishing website to review other Midwest history books in this series:

www.gbradleypublishing.com

ISBN 0-943963-87-7

Printed in the USA

DEDICATION
In honor of
Patricia Henry,
Illinois State Fair Historian

INTRODUCTION

The One Hundred Fiftieth anniversary of Illinois State Fair offers an opportunity to tell the story of Illinois' premier agricultural festival. Agriculture helped make Illinois one of the richest states in the nation and our state fair has been the stage on which the changing panorama of the state's agricultural development was traditionally displayed and celebrated. When the Illinois Agricultural Society proposed an annual fair in the 1850s to help educate farmers and advance farming methods, little could organizers have realized that it would grow to a major cultural and entertainment venue for the state. The small harvest festival grew not only into the state's most prominent agricultural event, but eventually brought world class entertainment, auto and harness racing and carnival thrills of every kind to visitors.

As Springfield historians in charge of the Sangamon Valley Collection at Lincoln Library, Springfield's public library, we were delighted, not only with the opportunity to research the history of Illinois' most important fair, but also one of Springfield's most venerable institutions. We discovered an embarrassment of riches in photographs and written and oral documentation. Our task was to sift through this mountain of materials to tell the story in words and pictures in 64 pages. Possibilities called to us from every side – Happy Hollow, crafts, racing, entertainment, food, historic buildings, politics, contests, horse shows, conservation activities, bake-offs, pony-tail and best baby contests, husband-calling, floral parades – and we knew from the beginning that the fair and all its rich past just couldn't be contained in these few pages. So we begin with an apology if we missed your favorite fair memory or activity. In the meantime we invite you to enjoy this look back on 150 wonderful years of the Illinois State Fair.

Dear Friends:

The Illinois State Fair is a celebration of our people, our culture and our heritage. Since 1853, Illinoisans have gathered annually to recognize the best our state has to offer in agriculture, machinery, technology, the culinary arts, racing competition and, of course, entertainment. The interests and achievements reflected in fair exhibits over the past 150 years have documented Illinois' progress from an undeveloped prairie to a diverse and economically powerful state.

It was with great pride that I commissioned this book to mark the fair's anniversary. Its pages chronicle not only the history of a glorious institution, but the history of Illinois as well.

Congratulations to Edward J. Russo, Melinda Garvert and Curtis Mann of Lincoln Library's Sangamon Valley Collection for so colorfully documenting the history of the Fair. Through the assistance of longtime State Fair Historian Patricia Henry, the authors have gathered a collage of anecdotes and pictures that demonstrate why the Illinois State Fair has become a must-attend summer tradition for millions of us over the past century and a half.

Sincerely,

George H Ryan

GEORGE H. RYAN
Governor of Illinois

Dear Fair goer:

I started showing Southdown sheep at the Illinois State Fair in the mid-1950s. And, like so many other rural Illinois families, the Fair has been a part of my life ever since.

As the State Fair has continued to grow and evolve over its long history, its heart has remained the same – agriculture. I have seen the carnival rides get bigger, the grandstand acts become huge productions of light and sound and the races get faster and faster. But, there is still no thrill on the fairgrounds that compares to the excitement of receiving a State Fair blue ribbon.

The pages that follow are a tribute to all of the people who have brought thrills to people, young and old, at the Illinois State Fair for the past 150 years. On behalf of the State Fair staff, I say thank you to the exhibitors, superintendents, vendors, racers, showmen, carnival operators, volunteers and the millions of visitors for a colorful and unmatched history in the celebration of agriculture.

Sincerely,

Joe Hampton

Joe Hampton
Director, Illinois Department of Agriculture

CHAPTER

I

Wandering Fair

Fairs in America are descendants of festivals of the Middle ages with their color, pageantry and excitement and entertainment of strolling jugglers, acrobats and musicians. But beyond entertainment, their purpose was a merchant's market—silks from the far east, furs from Russia and wool from Flanders. Our well-loved Illinois State Fair is a tribute to a remarkable institution that has adapted itself to needs and desires of the public through a century and a half of colossal change. At the fair's beginning in the 1850s agriculture was at the center of the state's economy and the majority of Illinois' population earned their livelihood from it. A great agricultural exhibit was then a major event. But today, with only a small percent of the population living on farms, the State Fair is still a major event on our annual calendar. While true to its agricultural roots, the fair has managed to grow and adapt to include also an extensive carnival attraction, big name entertainment, auto and motorcycle racing, and a plethora of food offerings along side traditional animal husbandry and farming exhibits. While a 19th century rural population, with few entertainment options, could be expected to patronize a state fair, it is a tribute to the Illinois State Fair's staying power that, today, with gigantic private amusement parks, television, movies, internet, inexpensive travel and a thousand other distractions, hundreds of thousands still enter the grounds every August. The fair's history reveals its amazing ability to remain popular through changing times in Illinois and the country for 150 years. The Illinois State Fair has been responsible for helping educate farmers to new methods and equipment and contributed directly to Illinois' rise to become a leading agricultural state.

Lord Chief Justice, a Cleveland Bay Stallion, was awarded a first premium at the 1888 state fair.

Twelve Illinois cities hosted the Illinois State Fair before Springfield was chosen as its permanent home. The 1856 State Fair was held in the city of Alton. This lithograph (right) provides a birds-eye view of the fairgrounds.

Until 1892 the fair was a movable feast, traveling around the state, with the idea of reaching wide audiences at a time when travel for rural families was difficult and expensive. The fair was founded as an educational institute at the time Illinois agriculture was first emerging. The 1830s marked the beginning of an incredible influx of settlers to the new state of Illinois. Virgin prairies were broken and turned to cropland. So great was production and vast the reach of these prairies that the term "corn belt" came to refer to the states of the central Midwest. During that same period the American Industrial Revolution was well underway, producing changes in agrarian life on a scale never before experienced. The primary change was the move from subsis-

tence farming to highly productive acreage aimed at a commercial market. Illinois' flat prairie lands were ideally suited to newly-invented reapers, mowers, planters and other implements that ushered in modern mechanized agriculture.

It was in this revolutionary period that the Illinois State Fair was born. Agricultural fairs in the United States originated in New York in the early 1800s and the first State Fair was held in Detroit, Michigan in 1849. The idea quickly took hold in Illinois where, in 1851, a public meeting open to all state farmers was held. This led eventually to the founding of the Illinois State Agricultural Society, ancestor of the state Department of Agriculture. The Society's first president, James N. Brown, Recording Secretary Simeon Francis and Treasurer, John Williams, were all from Springfield or Sangamon County and were deeply concerned that farmers were not advancing satisfactorily in their methods. This sentiment was strongly expressed in the very first volume of the Society's _Transactions_:

> However disagreeable to us, it must be confessed that, as a whole, home-bred farmers are necessarily among the most ignorant and big-oted members of the community. As they read little, and travel less, so has it been the more difficult to induce them to adopt improvements in their art…Education…they _do_ value, and usually at too big a rate. But not for themselves.

Society leaders decided that the best remedy was continuing education partly through a new agricultural fair to encourage the "best in field and garden crops, livestock, labor-saving implements and new ideas." It would also "help to elevate the individual farmer's opinion of his profession." Board members met in Springfield May 25, 1853 and voted to hold a fair that fall on the city's Sangamon County Fair Grounds. The first Illinois State Fair proved a great popular success and State Fair Historian Patricia Henry recounted the events of that first fair where "so many prized stallions, mares, colts, jacks and jennies, cattle, sheep, swine and poultry were entered that additional accommodations were hastily built." Altogether there were 765 individual entries with attendance ranging between fifteen and twenty thousand people by the third day and "not one inebriated man was seen!" Awards went to the best yoke of oxen, dairy products, fruit, grain, field crops including Illinois hemp and tobacco, garden produce, flowers, needlework, butter, baked goods, wines, artwork and hair wreaths. Visitors swarmed to that first fair with over 10,000 arriving in one day alone. There were the usual journalists' complaints comparing our's unfavorably with eastern fairs and one unkind remark about more swine roaming Springfield streets than were in pens on the fairgrounds.

Images Courtesy of Illinois State Historical Library

The second State Fair was held on the same site the following year but an outbreak of the dreaded cholera caused the date to be moved from September to October. The following year the fair began its annual migration around the state, playing a total of twelve cities until 1894 when it located permanently in Springfield. From the first the fair was such a prominent institution that there was hot competition among Illinois cities to play host. Exhibits of farm machinery, horses, poultry, livestock, grains, vegetables, household products and manufactured items continued to grow and made the fair **the state's single largest public event** and certainly the largest agricultural event in the state.

Almost from the first days popular amusements and entertainment vied with agriculture in drawing crowds. Horse racing, particularly harness racing, was the most important part of that entertainment early on. A general interest in horse racing began in the 1820s and 1830s and the first rules for the sport were drawn up in 1825. After 1830 trotting horses used harness and cart rather than racing under saddle, as previously. Harness racing easily captured the public's imagination because, according to one race historian, "anyone with a horse and buggy had engaged in a form of it on a country lane," rather like teens street-racing in their automobiles today. Harness racing was seen as everyman's sport. As America industrialized, city and country laborers no longer had the time for their own recreation and spectator sports became popular. Betting on the races quickly followed and states enacted laws making gambling illegal. But horse-race betting slipped through this virulent anti-gambling sentiment, especially after an 1830s Iowa case which held that horse racing was not a game of chance as defined in regulations and thus not forbidden by law. It would be the last years of the 19th century before opposition forces managed to get state laws enacted forbidding public betting on harness racing. However, State Fair racing was banned outright at least twice—in Quincy (1868) and Freeport (1877).

Still, the main emphasis in those early days was educational improvement —at least officially. The fairs were held in September and October, traditional harvest time, underscoring an agricultural emphasis. The fair went north to Chicago in 1855 and south to Alton in 1856 and more midstate at Peoria in 1857. The Centralia fair of 1858 exhibited two bulls named for the debating candidates Stephen Douglas and Abraham Lincoln. J.W. Fawkes, inventor, won a $3,000 prize for his steam plow, but had it taken back when it was discovered less perfect than "Mr. Fawkes designs to make it." But the real excitement came when balloonist Samuel Wilson gave a demonstration. When his passenger balloon landed in a nearby field, the farmer helped anchor it to a fence. Neighbors gathered and Mr. Wilson lifted the farmer's little girl and boy into the balloon's basket when suddenly it lifted off with the crying children aboard and their parents in a panic. An extra edition of the paper was published alerting the public. By morning the balloon descended and its anchor caught some trees about 18 miles away where the little boy was found asleep, wrapped in his sister's apron to keep warm.

During the Civil War in the 1860s several cities began coveting a role as permanent State Fair location. Decatur invested $15,000 in improvements to its fairgrounds, hoping to lure the fair there. In some cities price gouging of tourists was reported with Quincy's "lower class hotels [doubling] rates, better hotels more." New, improved sewing machines were some of the most popular exhibits of the decade as the busy housewife sought ways to save time. Premium categories expanded with awards for the best artificial teeth and limbs and women were first allowed to compete in horsemanship in 1868. Despite the fair's popularity, it was a continual financial battle for officials. For example in 1868 a financial disaster occurred when poor weather and horse race cancellations cut receipts almost in half.

The 1870s continued with expanding exhibits and added categories of animals. When DuQuoin hosted the exhibit in 1871 one reporter allowed that the exposition was "sure to do more toward modernizing lower Egypt [as southern Illinois was known] than anything that occurred in its history. That decade also saw the State Agricultural Society superceded by a new Department of Agriculture and State Fair Board. Back in Peoria in 1873, fairgoers were warned that the town was "full of gamblers, thieves, pickpockets and rogues generally, and faro banks blossomed out on every side." The year America celebrated its centennial, 1876, was one of the worst in the fair's first generation when the state legislature had to help pay premium awards due to a $13,000 deficit.

Peoria, despite its rogues, thieves and pickpockets, dominated as fair host in the 1880s and early 1890s, beating out Chicago as a close second, but tiny Olney in southeastern Illinois managed to capture it two years in a row—1887 and 1888. By 1890 the State Fair, and most county fairs were as associated with horse racing

Early fair farm machinery trials allowed manufacturers to show off their products and win premiums. Rugg's Reaper and Mower was awarded a diploma and $100 in 1857 at Salem, Illinois.

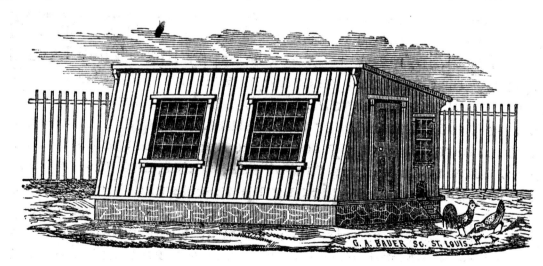

Farmers learned about the latest developments in agriculture at the state fair. Crop and animal improvements were featured along with new building ideas like this model poultry house.

and other popular amusements as they were with agricultural education and exhibits

By 1890, too, many state fairs in the country began to grow large, popular and tremendously successful, patterning their activities on the great international exhibitions of the 19th century. Though there had been earlier ones, Britain's Great Exhibition of 1851, held in London, was a milestone in attracting world wide attention to a single fair. It was immense in scale, both in activities and in construction. Its famous Crystal Palace—the first large-scale, prefabricated iron and glass building—was the centerpiece. The Paris International Exhibition of 1867 originated the idea of numerous exhibition buildings in a park-like setting, and the Paris Exhibition of 1889 – famed for its Eiffel Tower – carried those ideas even further. But it would be Chicago's World's Fair of 1892-3, the World's Columbian Exposition or "White City," which would dominate all previous exhibitions in concept, design, scale and execution. A completely new, neo-classical city was created by architects, artists, sculptors and landscape designers. Suddenly dreams of a permanent State Fair grounds of large-scale, classical exhibition halls set amid permanent landscaped surroundings emerged.

All of this was coming about as America urbanized and people leaving rural areas poured into cities. Frederick Jackson Turner famously stated that the "frontier" officially closed and there were no more pioneer places in the country. The country was described then as being on the one side "predominantly agricultural" with rural values, but rapidly becoming, on the other, "predominantly urban and industrial; inextricably involved in world economy and politics." And that emerging culture meant big changes for the Illinois State Fair.

As early as the 1870s agitation began for locating the fair permanently in one place. Improving, inexpensive rail transportation, common by the 1880s, made it possible for more Illinois people to go greater distances to a fair. This, combined with increasingly prohibitive costs of setting up new fairgrounds every few years, made State Agricultural Board members conclude that finding a permanent location "seemed reasonable." And, after 1870 the fair did not travel as far into the southern and northwestern parts of the state as earlier, but stayed instead generally in the more populated central and north-central regions.

The "new" Illinois State Fair would no longer be totally identified with agriculture, but, like the Columbian Exposition, would also promote manufacturing, scientific and industrial interests of an increasingly urban and industrial state. Marking its stylistic and physical connection to the Chicago exposition, were a large dome structure and four iron arches brought to Springfield from the Chicago fair. The arches were located in central Springfield and the dome re-erected at the fairgrounds. A new era had dawned for Illinois and its state fair.

1853-1892 Fair Locations

1853	Springfield	1874	Peoria
1854	Springfield	1875	Ottawa
1855	Chicago	1876	Ottawa
1856	Alton	1877	Freeport
1857	Peoria	1878	Freeport
1858	Centralia	1879	Springfield
1859	Freeport	1880	Springfield
1860	Jacksonville	1881	Peoria
1861	Chicago	1882	Peoria
1863	Decatur	1883	Chicago
1864	Decatur	1884	Chicago
1865	Chicago	1885	Chicago
1866	Chicago	1886	Chicago
1867	Quincy	1887	Olney
1868	Quincy	1888	Olney
1869	Decatur	1889	Peoria
1870	Decatur	1890	Peoria
1871	DuQuoin	1891	Peoria
1872	Ottawa	1892	Peoria
1873	Peoria		

No Fair:
1862 Peoria – Some premiums awarded but the military took over the fairgrounds for training (Civil War).
1893 Columbian Exposition Chicago World's Fair.
1942 thru 1945 U.S. Army uses fairgrounds (World War II).

A Home At Last

With permanent location in one city the Illinois State Fair entered into a period of remarkable growth with unprecedented amounts of money and attention lavished on its grounds. No fair was held in 1893 because of the state's heavy involvement with the Columbian Exposition. Late that year officials turned their attention to a permanent location. The process of site selection began with requirements sent to officials in cities interested in hosting the fair. Each city representative submitted an application and gave an oral pres-

entation at the Agriculture Department's board meeting in January 1894. The chief contenders were Bloomington, Decatur, Peoria and Springfield. Springfield finally won on the eighth ballot by offering the 156-acre grounds, construction of a fence and sewage system, free electric lights for two years, free city water forever (later rescinded) and $50,000 in cash. In addition to the cash incentive from Springfield, politicking in the General Assembly resulted in an astounding $225,000 appropriation for buildings.

Firebells, whistles and shouting greeted the news in Springfield. A flurry of activity followed as permanent buildings and other improvements were started. The grounds, formerly home to the Sangamon County Fair, were extensively altered. Department of Agriculture officials, according to a contemporary account, "did not attempt to build for the present: their foresight was employed for the benefit of those who are expected to enjoy and reap practical benefit from the Illinois State Fair for many years to come." In the first five years a series of impressive permanent buildings appeared beginning with the Exposition Building. One reporter sweepingly labeled it the

"…largest and best appointed building ever erected for a similar purpose in the United States." While perhaps overblown in his praise, the building is, never-the-less, an imposing structure. At its cornerstone laying July 4, 1894 the Masonic grand lodge of Illinois "…made an occasion of great moment" for the thousands attending. Machinery Hall, with its front octagonal bay, towered and limestone-trimmed brick design, was well underway before completion of the Exposition Building. Machinery Hall exhibits emphasized the rapidly changing methods of agriculture and so many new models of farm machinery were coming to market that officials found it difficult to provide display room in the main structure and resorted to tents nearby.

But the most dramatic structure on the grounds was, without a doubt, the Dome Building. The dome of the Columbian Exposition's Horticultural Hall,

A city of tents traditionally sprouts during the fair. This 1909 panoramic view of the northeast side of the state fairgrounds was taken from the Woman's Building.

then proclaimed to be the "second largest dome in the world, second only to the one on the Petrograd [later Leningrad] Cathedral in Russia," was transported to Springfield. The new building constructed for the dome was 200 by 200 feet. Beneath the "immense canopy of translucent glass" the dome gave "shelter to the fruits, vegetables, flowers, bees, honey, grains, seeds, pantry stores, dairy products" displays. In one corner of the immense main gallery alone, 1,000 chairs were set up almost un-noticed. The Dome Building went out in a blaze of glory when it burned in August 1917. An 8,000-seat grandstand (replaced by the present one in 1927) a one mile dirt track, 25 horse barns, swine, cow and sheep exhibition barns, public dining hall, Poultry (now Artisans) Building and a half-dozen small service buildings were all complete before 1900. Seven entrances gave access to the grounds that, at the time, stretched only between Peoria Road and the 8th Street gate. When the new fair opened 1894 gate admission was free the first day resulting in a

swarm of visitors. After that admission was 50 cents, quite a sum in those days. Seventy-five cents was charged for one person on horseback, but only 50 cents for a two-horse vehicle (which was presumably less likely to speed than a young man on a horse, hence its lower fee). A little girl, Harriet Neal, was the winner of the first Illinois State Fair baby contest that year because she was the only baby not crying.

Newspapers in several Illinois communities complained bitterly about the fair being permanently encamped in one city, never to visit others. But a Springfield booster, comparing gate receipts from the first year, said that the new fair "achieved greater success the first year in its permanent location that it ever reached during its peregrinations over the state, verifying all the expectations of those who contended that it must find a permanent home, or go out of existence."

The traditional agricultural education emphasis of crop, livestock and implement exhibits and demonstrations was clearly still central to the fair, as it had been for 40 years. But popular entertainment was already gaining a strong foothold by the 1890s and would begin to challenge agriculture's supremacy. Horse racing and betting activities connected with it were still the largest entertainment draw. Despite the growing opposition to gambling, horse racing was now prominently featured. A mile track was constructed and the Agriculture board encouraged running of noted horses there. A brochure of the time predicted it would "become one of the greatest places for race meets in the country," with "the finest grandstand in the western country." The buildings for the horses were referred to as "speed barns" with everything built for safety and

BARNEY OLDFIELD.

"BEACHEY WINS"

One popular attraction at the 1914 State Fair was a race held on the track between aviator Lincoln Beachy and driver William Endicott (misidentified in the photo as "Barney Oldfield"). Beachy is shown here in his winning airplane.

convenience. In 1897 the horse Star Pointer set a new record of 2:005 for the mile.

A midway, located adjacent to the grandstand and complete with sideshow barkers, an Electric Lady, talking pony, fortune tellers and a snake charmer, had edged in by 1896 despite much heated discussion about compromising the fair's moral and uplifting atmosphere. Until 1907, however, perhaps in an effort to maintain that dignified and moral tone, other carnival activities were prohibited from the grounds. They were instead held on the downtown public square where the arches brought from the Chicago World's Fair and the Courthouse were outlined in electric lights, then a great rarity. Souvenir tents and novelty and refreshment stands lined the streets on the four sides of the square. By 1907 demand had grown strong enough so that the carnival was permitted on the fairgrounds and discontinued downtown. The carnival was assigned a sunken grassy area at the south side of the Exposition Building christened "Happy Hollow." Here until 1996, (and except for a few years in the 1970s), the carnivals, rides and sideshows of the fair were located. A second, permanent amusement area with children's rides (near the giant slide) was developed just inside the Main Gate in the 1950s.

The new twentieth century marked continued agricultural growth in Illinois, and was the first period of general prosperity for Illinois farmers since the Civil War era. There had been a fall in commodities prices as competition from the newly-opened northwest flooded the country with farm products. The 1880s and '90s were generally hard times for state farmers and it took until about 1900 before reports of the Illinois State Board of Agriculture again indicated farmers making steady profits. The fair, the largest agricultural event in the state, reflected these improving economic conditions. Building projects continued with completion of the Coliseum in 1902, the Dairy Building in 1903, Fire House about 1905, Sheep and Swine Pavilions in 1909 and 1912, Show Horse Barns in 1913 and dozens of other horse and cattle barns, service buildings and curbs, lighting, sewers and concrete walks. The "Haskall Viaduct for foot passengers is a graceful structure of iron spanning the roadway between the Poultry and Exposition build-

A relaxing couple survey the excitement of Happy Hollow about 1914. Happy Hollow became the site of the fair's carnival rides, games and sideshows in 1907.

ings...one of the picturesque features of the landscape," according to the 1900 Premium Catalog. Financially things improved as well. A 1912 report compared premiums and gate receipts for the second decade of the permanent fair with those of the first. In 1910 attendance was nearly 334,000 compared with a little over 177,000 in 1894 and premiums of almost $57,000 had more than doubled in the same time period. New machinery was being eagerly snapped up by farmers, and the 518 machinery exhibits of 1894 had jumped to an amazing 7,370 by 1911. An old school building next to the main entrance was purchased and became the fair director's home.

The tradition of variously-themed "days" was soon established. Monday was School Children's Day, Tuesday Exhibitors" Day, Wednesday Old Soldiers" (later Veterans') Day , Thursday Governor's Day and Friday Floral Parade when carriages decked out with flowers made a procession to the grounds. Saturday was Springfield Day when businesses closed for the afternoon so employees could attend. Capitalizing on the passion for educational exhibits, the Sears Roebuck Company erected the Sears Pavilion in 1909. A complete bungalow was built as the second floor of a building filled with home furnishings. Everything, including the bungalow itself, could be purchased through the Sears catalog. The house was later lowered and is today the fair manager's home.

1902 marked the 50th anniversary of the Illinois State Fair, which was marred by loss of the Women's Building soon replaced by a new brick structure demolished in 1973. A special streetcar service began in 1904 bringing a car a minute from downtown. The Illinois Traction System's interurban railroad lines entered the grounds and transported visitors from all across the state. These early years of the 20th century gave birth to another form of popular entertainment as well. Automobile racing joined horse racing on the mile track. As early as 1905 famous pioneer race driver Barney Oldfield had included the fair on his barnstorming circuit with his Green Dragon racing car. By 1910 regular auto races were a part of the venue. That year Oldfield had a stunt race with an airplane and Springfield driver LaRue Vredenburgh was killed when his car crashed. Events of national significance in auto racing occurred at the Fairgrounds on both the old and present (1927) track. In the 1930s the fair's first American Automobile Association's 100 mile National Championship race was held, making national news. The Springfield track remains dirt, while most others on the circuit have been paved over. It is still a famously fast auto and motorcycle track.

By the time of the first World War many fair buildings were 25 years old and in need of their first major repairs and, despite labor and material short-

Horse racing – harness and running – have been part of the fair from the first. Here harness racers cross the finish line in front of the original grandstand in the 1890s.

ages during the war, some rehabilitation projects were underway. During 1918, the last year of the war, Illinois celebrated its centennial and former President Theodore Roosevelt was invited to make an address. The admission price of 50 cents with horseback price of 75 cents remained unchanged since 1894 but a new category, automobiles, were admitted for 50 cents as well. "Big Charley," the world's largest purebred Shorthorn, weighing 4,180 pounds, was displayed at the 1918 fair. Amateur motorcycle races were held and entertainment included a Grand Industrial Parade, Sacred Concert, Weil's Chicago Orchestra, Auto Polo, Greater Centennial Circus, Baby Health Contest, Liberati's Concert Band with Sixteen Grand Opera Singers, Capitol City Band, Million Dollar Livestock Parade and Old Settlers Day.

Great changes came to the fair after the war. It was a time of updating and revitalization for the fairgrounds. In 1920 the grounds' poor physical condition and lack of novelty in offerings contributed to a waning public interest. "Circumstances in recent years," admitted fair manager B.M. Davison, "have tended to decrease the attendance somewhat." An administrative reorganization was a first step in changing the fair to reflect new times. From being just a unit of the state Agricultural Department, the fair was made a separate state institution with its own advisory board and appropriations. The advisory board was fortunate to have as its chair Len Small of Kankakee, a former state treasurer and future governor (1921-1929). Small is credited with modernizing Illinois' highway system and is remembered as Illinois' "Hard Roads Man." Under his vigorous leadership, Illinois

Visitors stroll from the main gate towards the Exposition Building in 1897 when the grounds were only a few years old. Courtesy of Illinois State Historical Library

literally pulled itself out of the mud by instituting a wide-ranging system of paved highways and secondary roads. Small was also an expert at promoting expansion of state programs and buildings, particularly the State Fair. Under his leadership the fair's dates of operation were moved from September and October back to August. This symbolized the change from accommodating primarily the farmer who had free time after harvest, to catering to the city, town and non-farming rural residents during their traditional summer holiday. The non-farming public now made up a greater share of fair visitors and would demand continually more and livelier entertainment beyond traditional cattle and machinery shows.

One of Small's acts as Governor was to secure clear title to the 156-acre fairground for the state, which had been previously held subject to certain provisions. At the same time he successfully negotiated purchase of an additional 210 acres immediately west of the 8th Street gate running west to 5th Street, bringing the grounds to the current 366 acres. The former 8th Street was then enclosed part of the grounds. Most buildings were refurbished by 1925 and a number of service buildings and new barns put up. Roads were paved and electricity, sewers, fencing and general streetscape improvements made.

A major building program took place during Governor Small's second term. Next to a full-page photo of the governor the 1928 State Fair Premium Book extolled these planned and completed changes:

> With the transfers completed and the titles recorded, construction was begun on a…race course and grandstand, both of which were dedicated during the 1927 Fair…1928 will see the dedication of 6 new cattle barns, a new machinery field and completion of a new 8 foot steel fence around the entire property.

A 30 year old clubhouse for Springfield's private Sangamo Club was demolished and the newly expanded grounds would "welcome visitors with its most beautiful offering of trees, shrubs, grass and flowers."

Small's successor, Louis Lincoln Emerson, launched a $2.5 million state building program that included many new fair structures, among them a Women's Building, known officially as the Emmerson Building. The new State Architect, C. Herrick Hammond, who would remain responsible for fair buildings until 1952, designed the Emmerson and had a guiding hand in grounds development for that entire generation.

By the 1930s the entertainment aspect of the fair began to be honestly acknowledged. Harness racing grew rapidly in popularity. In his report to the fair-going public in 1931, Governor Emmerson promised that, "While the Fair is primarily educational, it has not and will not neglect to provide wholesome amusement." And indeed, the fair during the 1930s focused on broad-based, popular entertainment. Better Babies contests, motorcycle races, dance bands, hog calling contests, live radio broadcasts, airplane shows, beer gardens, fashion parades and auto displays became more and more prominent in promotional publications. The Beckmann & Garety Shows, which billed themselves as the world's largest midway, were contracted to replace earlier, less elaborate carnivals in Happy Hollow. Beckmann boasted an array of modern mechanical rides. A series of professionally produced films promoting the State Fair were distributed throughout the Midwest in the mid-1930s and early 1940s. These stressed amusement and escapist themes as much or more than those of agriculture and education. By 1939 fair officials even had begun reaching out to various ethnic groups with folk dancing displays and a well promoted Boccie Ball Tournament. Professional "Revues" featured famous talent, and later individual big name acts came to the grandstand stage.

All of this promotion of the fair as entertainment was clearly in touch with public demand and made the exposition a popular success. State Fair Manager E.E. Irwin proudly reported that the 1937 Fair "had an attendance of more than a million—the largest of any state fair in the entire country." These record attendance figures remained at this level for the next decades and officials had difficulty breaking them even by the 1970s and 1980s.

The 1940 fair opened the new decade with a flourish, celebrating "Youth Day the American Way," appropriately patriotic with war rumblings in the background. William V. "Jake" Ward succeeded E.E. Irwin in 1941 and his first fair, recalled by State Fair Historian Patricia Henry, offered the WLS National Barn Dance, the Hoosier Hotshots, grandstand performance by Orrin Tucker with Bonnie Baker, Horace Heidt and Ted Weems orchestras and a trained dog show. But with America's entry into war after Pearl Harbor the fair was cancelled for the duration of the war. The United States War Department occupied the grounds until spring 1946. With rushed preparations a full fair reopened that August complete with most entertainment, contests and exhibits joined by a new "Homemakers Institute for War Brides." The following year "fan" dancer Sally Rand and stripper Georgia Sothern made headlines, drawing large crowds and enough notoriety to be banned from future appearances. The Typical Farm Family Contest was among programs dropped as the fair entered its 99th year. But the most significant fair of the century was on the immediate horizon—the 100th anniversary fair of 1952.

A large crowd works its way past a number of tents pitched in front of the Woman's Building in 1905. Many of the tents provided food for the hungry visitors. Courtesy of Illinois State Historical Library

*T*his 1921 aerial view shows the Illinois State Fairgrounds as they looked before the major remodeling project of 1927-28. Looking east from Sangamon Avenue, Machinery Hall is seen in the foreground.

*Q*uilts and bedspreads along with afghans, embroidery, smocking, and crochet work filled display cases from the first days of the fair.

*T*he premium was $2.50 in the yeast bread category in 1947 but the look on this winner's face is the real prize—the joy of winning a blue ribbon.

*P*oultry judges slowly work their way down the long row of cages, carefully inspecting each bird to determine a state fair champion.

McMeen's Taffy Candy

10¢,15¢,25¢&50¢ BAGS
75¢ BOXES

MCMEENS TAFFY
POST WWII
FIRST TRAILER

BUDWEISER

PREFERRED *Everywhere*

BUDWEISER
THE KING OF BOTTLED BEER
PREFERRED *Everywhere*

PREFERRED *Everywhere*

SNOW BALL

*M*cMeen's Taffy Candy, one of the many family-owned stands that returned annually, is shown in this 1946 photo with the first trailer used by the family at the state fair.

*B*eer tents were a popular stop in the late 1930s through the early 1950s. Beer came to the fairgrounds in 1933, was banned in 1953 and returned in 1974.

*T*he dairy bar inside the Dairy Building was a mandatory stop for visitors wanting to cool off with milk, sundaes and shakes. These smiling attendants kept the ice cream rolling in 1949.

These six beef and dairy cattle barns were part of a major building program undertaken in 1928 during the administration of Governor Len Small.

*T*he Rambouillet was just one of 11 different breeds of sheep judged at the state fair in the late 1930s. This handler has his ram well groomed and ready for showing.

*S*pectators give wide berth to this string of Angus show cattle being led across the fairgrounds in 1947.

*B*occie Ball was brought to the United States by Italian immigrants. Tournaments were held at the state fair starting in 1939. Here a player tosses the ball during a match.

The thought of a frothy mug of root beer for 5 cents tempted many fairgoers. Tony R. Berrettini, Superintendent of Concessions in the 1930s, had his own stand shown here.

Attention to grooming, for both animals and their handlers, was an important aspect of competition. This nattily-dressed, cigar-biting trainer of the old school holds his prize-winning horse in 1919.

Pacer Star Pointer's win over Joe Patchen in 1897 gave the fair track its first recognition as a "fast track." The original track seen here was relocated to its present site in 1927.

WORLDSRACE RECORD
STAR POINTER 200½

*H*arness racing has often filled Grandstand seating to near capacity as shown here in 1947. The Illinois State Fair is a part of the Grand Circuit of horse racing.

*D*rivers hunch low behind their handle bars during motorcycle races held at the fair of 1911.

Two prize winning swine, recently sold, are paraded around the fairgrounds in the early 1930s. Champion livestock were often purchased by state celebrities or officials like Governor Henry Horner as shown here.

Junior Department
Grand Champion Barrow
Exhibited By
Norbert Brunner
Sangamon County

Grand Champion Barrow
PURCHASED BY
GOV. HORNER
at 2.00 per POUND
Exhibited by
ARNOLD MOORE, Union City, Okla.

HERBERT GEORG STUDIO #5

Different breeds of beef cattle and their handlers were photographed in 1928 with the brand new Grandstand building as a backdrop.

This proud young man with his two heifer calves shows the emphasis on encouraging future farmers through 4-H and junior livestock competitions.

Getting lost at the fair can be a terrifying experience for kids. Luckily Illinois State Policemen assist in reuniting family members like this little lost girl in the 1940s.

The kids must be fed at the fair as on the farm. Here the does (mother goats) involved in milking competition are getting a little human help feeding their kids.

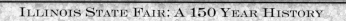

State agencies often set up booths at the state fair, providing the public with information about their government. These visitors inspect the Department of Public Works and Buildings display in 1949.

Fairgoers, at the Centennial fair in 1952 amble past rows of tents housing perennial occupants from beer gardens to seed corn dealers and food vendors to retailers.

Dairy cows and their handlers stand patiently beneath a field of colorful banners during a judging session inside the Coliseum building in the 1940s.

CHAPTER

III

A Changing Image

Nostalgia for the past was not much in evidence for the fair's 100th anniversary celebration in 1952. A series of articles in Springfield's *Illinois State Register* newspaper played up fair history and smilingly recalled stories about early fairs like the Chicago newspapers warning rural folk to beware of "slick tongued" conmen, or how Springfield had to fill the holes in the streets made by roaming hogs before its first fair in 1853. But mostly the emphasis was on the world of tomorrow. With memories of war, depression and other hard times so recently in mind, people wanted to look forward, not backward. One writer, recalling those first years of the '50s, described that Korean War era's "pessimism and foreboding," with fair news relinquishing "its usual top mid-summer spot [on] Springfield news pages" to war reports. Escapism, in the form of "huge beer tents," were crowded until after midnight "as a war-scarred generation drank away to blur the unhappy thought of a return to the barracks and troopship."

Beef cattle are paraded in front of the Department of Public Safety's tent during the 1950 state fair.

On the surface the Centennial fair of 1952 looked much like those of the previous years with its contests, animals, racing and midway rides. But change—in the grounds and entertainment—was the keynote of the day. The fair in the 1950s would be all about being up-to-date, reflecting a country entering the age of space travel, transistor radios and the dawning of computer technology. The most "spectacular" event of the 1952 fair featured the most potent symbol of change—a procession of the latest model automobiles parading the grounds.

Manager H.W. Elliott proudly reported to the press that the value of grounds and buildings was $7 million, and annexation of the grounds to the city of Springfield was proposed. But most other news releases and stories in the early '50s focused on modernization of an aging fairgrounds. A new bandstand (where much of the folk dancing for today's Ethnic Village takes place) was completed in 1953. Governor William Stratton approved a study for a proposed new Coliseum to handle overflowing horse show crowds, and a new feed and fertilizer testing lab was begun. The Conservation Area was completely refurbished and new exhibits presented. The buffalo on those grounds were descendants of ones from the old Springfield Zoo and Amusement Company that had once been located nearby. But the most notable physical change was the new Illinois Building near the main gate, first

A marching band passes through the 1910 main gate at the fairgrounds during the Twilight Parade. Twilight parades began in 1984.

opened for the 1950 fair. The International Style building represented a clear departure with the past and the Classical Revival designs of the rest of the grounds. The post-war fairs were clearly aiming for modernity in look and mood. A high point of the 1954 fair was a visit by President Dwight D. Eisenhower, the first president since Rutherford B. Hayes to speak at the fair while in office.

Television, in its infancy in 1950, would, by the end of the decade, give serious competition to other entertainment including the Illinois State Fair. Millions of viewers could now see big name entertainment without leaving the comfort of their living rooms. A first-ever nationwide television broadcast from the fair was made in 1955. To counter declining attendance fair planners began recruiting more popular entertainment for the Grandstand. Previously a band or popular singer like Rudy Vallee would perform at the Grandstand on Saturday night. On other evenings local talent, the WLS Barn Dance, choruses and the like filled in. By the mid 1950s the popular "Holiday on Ice" ice skating extravaganza became an annual feature. But it was the last years of the decade when fair shows began to directly reflect television culture. Headliners included Hugh O'Brian, Dodie Stevens, Ed "Kookie" Burns, Hugh Downs, James Garner and others made famous by TV. The WLS Barn Dance was replaced in 1959 by the Grand Ole Opry show on the first Saturday night of the fair which brought legendary stars Patsy Cline, Tex Ritter, Roy Acuff, Waylon Jennings, Minnie Pearl, George Jones and Hank Williams, Jr. to the State Fair stage.

Press reports then continually stressed everything "modern" about the fair. Typical were quotes like "The Sputnik and missile age [are] reflected in today's sleek exhibits of military rockets." And a decidedly non-agricultural emphasis was tried. The fair, we learned, "…was to mirror the change in attitudes of Midwestern Americans who came to realize they are part of a new era…" In that long era of post-war peace and prosperity a typical visitor was "more likely to be concerned about meeting a payment on his air conditioner than the possible arrival of a draft notice."

Beer sales on the grounds were banned by executive order of Governor William Stratton in 1953. A big feature during the fairs was the Illinois Department of Public Health's Chest-X-RAY program that offered free X-rays to the general public and all state fair food handlers. The "Gainer Lasses" were a couple of women in Lil' Abner-style outfits sitting on a fence and Frank Dutt's butter cow was one of the most popular exhibits in those last years of the 1950s.

While changes were inevitable due to public demand, it was also true that the heart of the fair—agriculture and politics—remained firmly in place, not subject to the whims of taste despite a renewed emphasis on popular entertainment. A 1959 story amuses with its self-assured announcement that "State Fair politics, which reached a peak with the 1954 visit here of President Eisenhower, have become a casualty dispensed with in 1956, with no sign they will ever return." Little did the writer realize how vital are politics to a state fair.

By the 1960s a new, more serious tone came back to the fair. Youth in agriculture was highlighted, and a "scientific" approach to everything from farming to education was in evidence. Such a serious, educational approach had hardly been present in fair promotions since the early days of the State Agricultural Society and may have been linked in part to our fear of the USSR's perceived superiority in the space race. News releases spoke of the fair's becoming "a more serious agricultural and scientific exposition in the Surging '60s, "mirroring the achievements that science and industry ensure for a booming decade." A casual aside in one story noted that "the emphasis on youth will continue in the opening years of the new decade." But, fair officials probably had no idea how much young people would be courted as the baby boom grew from toddlers to teens.

The 1962 fair premiered Farm-A-Rama which marked the return of major agricultural equipment exhibits including International Harvester, John Deere, Oliver, Massey-Ferguson, J.I. Case, New Idea, New Holland and Moline. Live agriculture demonstrations were offered every few hours. Twenty-three of the Midwest's top entertainers were featured with evening dancing. State leaders of the National Farm Organization, National Grange, American Farm Association and other agricultural organizations appeared. New Fair Director Franklin Rust promised to "return the agriculture atmosphere to the Illinois State Fair" and "1962 will see us regain our top position as the World's Greatest Agricultural Exposition." But the space age was there as well with a NASA exhibit, Nuclear Exhibit from Oak Ridge, Tennessee and the Naval Electronics display. There was an ominous side of life in a nuclear world seen in a popular, and permanent "bomb shelter" exhibit. Radio disc jockey Jim Harry spent several days inside to demonstrate how it might work. The Illinois Industrial Showcase was added in the 1960s to highlight made-in-Illinois products and "Women's World" exhibits were enlarged.

The Illinois State Legislature released funds to continue refurbishing grounds and buildings. Plans for a new women's building, swine pavilion, extensive landscaping and mechanically updating older structures were included in a $2 million expansion program. Nearly $1 million was spent on a new Junior Livestock building, livestock barns, Coliseum roof and other upgrades. But many other buildings and facilities were still in sadly deteriorating condition, a fact not hidden by this beginning facelift. The old Machinery Hall was deemed "very dangerous, and foretold of demolitions of early fair buildings that would take place in the coming decade.

An extra day was added to the 1964 fair which was billed as an eleven day extravaganza featuring a statewide music festival, competitive categories for marching bands, stage bands and baton twirling. A Teen-age Fair with

A state police officer speaks into his radio (lower right) as people stand on their cars in the racetrack infield to watch a procession of antique automobiles pass by in 1954.

ILLINOIS STATE FAIR: A 150 YEAR HISTORY

Miss Teen-age contest, beauty contests, cars, fashion shows and nightly entertainment drew young people in large numbers. An Old West "Ghost" town featured bank robberies, shootings, and a concert hall with continuous entertainment. It was planned to change the Grandstand stage show nightly, Tuesday through Saturday, which made a profit for the first time in several years. When attendance that year topped one million it was front page news. A Boccie Ball Tournament, coon hound and stock horse shows highlighted the last day of the fair and Phil Hazenfield's "Casuals" group from Decatur won the Governor's Trophy and a cash prize in a statewide Rock 'n Roll contest. Nearly 140,000 attendees jammed the grounds on Veterans Day that year.

Teen audiences proved so lucrative that the next year the "Young America Fair" was a main attraction with fun for the "young at heart," including cheerleading contests, custom cars, cosmetics, records, athletic equipment a Battle of the Bands, Hootenany Hullaballoo, "and numerous other talent acts." The emphasis on youth mentioned in press releases was evident at this special fair-within-a-fair, but also throughout the entire grounds. The fair was trying to appeal especially to teens to increase its attendance. But many fair rules still emphasized traditional values. For example, requirements for ushering at the grandstand were clear cut. "Men must be six feet tall, at least 16 years old, can't have mustaches or long hippie haircuts, and have pleasant personalities and the maturity to meet any situation." For girls it was easier, they had to be "pretty and pleasant."

Still, despite appeal to free-spending teens, newly-landscaped grounds and big name entertainment, fair attendance peaked or even dropped slightly. The 1966 Fair, while financially successful, was marred by a weekend of tragedy when a 14-foot section of iron and timber catwalk, weighing about a ton, fell 100 feet from the roof of the grandstand into a crowd of racing fans, killing three persons and injuring 30 others. A motorcyclist was also killed and two others critically injured in that year's race.

In 1967 the Swiss cable sky ride was begun and the giant steel statue of Abe Lincoln by sculptor Carl Rinnus became permanent parts of the grounds.

When Illinois celebrated its Sesquicentennial in 1968 twelve huge red, white and blue seals decorated the grounds and were visible to motorists traveling along Sangamon Avenue. But the most lasting legacy from that year was the giant slide, one of the more famous bits of architecture on the grounds. The big news at that fair was lack of space for animals. Record numbers of livestock were shown. Hogs were doubled up in barns, tents were built to hold sheep and "the goat barn was filled with the largest registration in the history of the fair." Quarter horses overran their housing and were kept in area barns, with 700 entered in the races as compared with 30 in 1961. Manager Rust resigned before the 1969 fair to become manager of the famed Busch Gardens in Tampa, Florida. Rust had served nearly the entire decade of the '60s but in the next decade six managers would come and go.

The 1970s opened with a troubling story when Gov. Richard Ogilvie announced a probe of wrong-doing by fair officials, and that as many as eight indictment might be made. The scandal culminated in 1974 with at least one firing and new financial procedures. The scandal hung over the fair like a dark cloud with one Springfield newspaper calling the affairs of the State Fair Agency "a fiscal mess." Despite continual pressure to remove the fair from direct control by the Illinois Governor, it took until 1979, after several years of political wrangling, before the Fair Agency was merged with the Illinois Department of Agriculture. The new agency was the Division of Fairs and Horse Racing.

Throughout the '70s, under various directors the State Fair searched for its identity in changing times. Themes ran from "Come Smile With Us," (1972-73), "Super-Fair" (1975) to "A Family-A-Fair" (1977) and "Around the World in Eleven Days (1978)." In an effort to draw larger crowds the Coliseum, Children's World and Grandstand (except auto racing) shows were free in 1973 and the Lincoln Stage opened. The following year admission was reduced from $1.50 to $1.00 for adults, but most surprisingly, beer made a comeback and was allowed on the grounds for the first time in 20 years. In 1977 the breathtaking sight of giant hot air balloons hovering over the grounds signaled the first balloon race at the fair in over a century. A new Aviation World featured home-built airplanes. Grandstand entertainment in those years ranged from Captain & Tennille, K.C. & the Sunshine Band, Johnny Cash, Charley Pride and Glen Campbell to England Dan & John Ford Coley, Jim Nabors, Doc Severinsen, Bobby Goldsboro and the Grand Ole Opry with Tammy Wynette.

But all the entertainment changes could not disguise the fact that the grounds and buildings were aging. Deferred maintenance had put many of the buildings in poor condition. Some were demolished rather than rehabilitated as a cost saving measure. The old Textile Building, once the base above which the Sears Bungalow was suspended, was demolished in 1971. The Administration (former Women's) Building and Machinery Hall, a landmark from the first days, were both demolished in 1973. The Goat Barn burned in 1976. Conditions were bad enough in many remaining buildings to cause public embarrassment. Boys State decided the physical condition of the Junior Home Economics Building was so deplorable they cancelled in 1974

A traditional Parade of Champions passes in front of the Grandstand in 1957.

"Watseka Wanda," a Berkshire sow, was the first grand champion for Charles E. White of Watseka, Illinois. Wanda had an eight-pig litter before winning her class.

for the first time in over 60 years. Leaking roofs, broken glass, rot and dirt plagued many structures.

Lieutenant Governor Neil Hartigan wanted to call out the Illinois National Guard to remedy the situation—literally. He suggested that the guard could work on the buildings during weekends and summer encampments.

But a new spirit seemed to move through the fair with the upcoming American Revolution Bicentennial in 1976. A revived interest in preserving and renovating many of the historic structures took hold. The landmark Exposition Building, the first permanent building on the grounds, was restored at the beginning of a $2.9 million renovation program. Years of paint were removed and the mellow tone of brick contrasted once more with sparkling, freshly-painted trim. Rehabilitation of the old Poultry Barn, renamed the Artisans Building, followed, and the Main Gate was restored to its original beauty. A new Department of Agriculture headquarters building was planned and the Swine Pavilions were re-roofed and improved. "We want to restore the fairgrounds to what we think it basically looked like when it was started," said one fair administrator at the time.

As America entered her second century, the Illinois State Fair clearly reflected the monumental changes that had taken place in agriculture—from horse and mule power to mechanized machinery, hybrid seeds, and the coming of agri-business and helping the family farm survive. "Now that farming is so technologized," said one newspaper, "the state fair is no longer the place where farmers swap seeds, stock and secrets." "But," asked Griggsville-area farmers J.B. and Kathleen Baxter, who faithfully attended 40 years of fairs, "How do you get educated too?" The question was a legitimate one, for, despite all the change in the fair—entertainment at the forefront and growth

*T*he Society Horse Show is a national championship competition held in the Coliseum. The light horse classes feature walking, 3-gaited and, here, 5-gaited horses as well as horses and ponies in harness.

of horse and auto racing, merchandising and technological wonders exhibits— the fair was still a place where many farmers turned to learn the latest changes affecting their work.

More and more the Fair's (and America's) heritage was appreciated as the 20th century drew to a close. A Heritage Square was the beginning of the Ethnic Village, celebrating our country's diverse cultures. Increasingly themes like "The Good Old Days" appeared in fair publicity in the 1980s. And public appreciation and affection for this venerable institution became obvious. "Illinois State Fair rich in history, pageantry," headlined a story in the *Illinois Agri-News* paper. The fair even got its own unofficial historian, Patricia Henry, a Springfield resident and loyal fair-goer for over 50 years. By the mid-1980s attendance again topped one million. Capitalizing on its tradition helped return the fair to a high level of popularity. The familiar color, sights, sounds, smells and feel of the fair were summed up in a Department of Agriculture description from the 1980s:

Willie Nelson, balloon races, 950 lb pigs, bands, corn dogs, horse races, cotton candy, husband calling, honey ice cream, a butter cow sculpture, huge farm machinery, beer tents, canoe rides, smiling queens, handshaking politicians, bake-offs, batons twirling, fireworks and fast cars – all this and more can be found at the Illinois State Fair.

These and so much more have made the Illinois State Fair a blue ribbon winner for the State of Illinois and its people for 150 years.

*W*ith paper and pencil in hand, this group of young men closely inspect a selection of beef calves during a judging contest.

ILLINOIS STATE FAIR LEADERSHIP

State Fair Presidents/Directors

Illinois State Agricultural Society

(< notes conflicting information)

1853-54 James Brown
1855 Harvey Johns
1857-58 Cyrus Webster
1859-60 Lewis Ellesworth
1861-64 Wm. Van Epps
1865-68 A.B. McConnell
1869-70 William Kile
1871-72 David Brown

Illinois State Board of Agriculture formed

1873 David Brown<
1874 John Reynolds<
1875-78 D.B. Gillham
1879-82 J.R. Scott
1883-86 John Landrigan
1887-88 Samuel Dysart
1889-90 George Haskell
1891-92 Lafayette Funk
1893-94 David Gore
1895-96 James Judy
1897-98 J. Irving Pearce
1899-00 Wm. Fulkerson
1901-02 Martin Conrad
1903-04 James Dirkirson
1905-06 A.D. Barber
1907-07 George Madden
1909-10 John Crebs
1911-12 George Anthony<
1913-14 J.T. Montgomery
1915 J.K. Hopkins<
1916 Len Small<
1917-18 J.E. Taggart

An Illinois State Fair Agency is formed

Directors of Agriculture

1919-20 Charles Adkins
1921-24 B.M. Davison
1925-28 Stillman Stanard
1929 Clarence Buck
1930-32 Stuart Pierson
1933-36 Walter McLaughlin
1937-40 J.H. Lloyd
1941 Howard Leonard
No fair during WW II
1946-48 Arnold Benson
1949-52 Roy Yung
1953-60 Stillman Stanard
1961-62 Ralph Bradley
1963-68 Robert Schneider
1969 John Lewis
1970-72 Gordon Ropp
1973-76 Robert Williams
1977-80 John Block

State Fair Agency becomes the Division of Fairs & Horse Racing under the Department of Agriculture in 1979

1981-89 Larry Werries
1990 Jack Rundquist
1991-98 Becky Doyle
1999-present Joe Hampton

State Fair Managers

1919-20 B.M. Davison
1921-29 Walter Lindley
1930-32 Milton Jones
1933-34 Edward Collins
1935-39 E.E. Irwin
1941 Jake Ward
No fair during WW II
1946 Jake Ward
1947-48 Jake Ward & Arnold Benson
1949-52 H.J. White
1953 James Tays
1954-56 Strother Jones
1957-60 J. Ralph Peak
1961-68 Franklin Rust
1969 Raymond Phipps
1970 John Kadow (Interim)
1971 Thomas Evans
1972-73 Bob Park
1974-76 Paul King
1977-78 Nick Stone
1979 Nick Alexander
1980-83 Sid Hutchcraft
1984-90 Merle Miller
1991-94 Bud Hall
1995-98 Joe Saputo
1999-present Bud Ford

Governors of Illinois

1853-56 Joel Matteson
1857-59 William Bissell
1860 John Wood
1861-64 Richard Yates
1865-68 Richard Oglesby
1869-72 John Palmer
1873-76 John Beveridge
1877-82 Shelby Cullom
1883-84 John Hamilton
1885-88 Richard Oglesby
1889-92 Joseph Fifer
1893-96 John Altgeld
1897-00 John Tanner
1901-04 Richard Yates
1905-12 Charles Deneen
1913-16 Edward Dunne
1917-20 Frank Lowden
1921-28 Len Small
1929-32 Louis Emmerson
1933-40 Henry Horner
1941-48 Dwight Green
1949-52 Adali Stevenson
1953-60 William Stratton
1961-67 Otto Kerner
1968 Samuel Shapiro
1969-72 Richard Ogilvie
1973-76 Dan Walker
1977-90 Jim Thompson
1991-98 Jim Edgar
1999-present George Ryan

People wait to board a bus providing rides around the fairgrounds. Others choose to walk the grounds. This crowded thoroughfare is lined with the flags of many countries.

These racecars kick up dirt as they round the curve at the 1975 state fair. The fairgrounds is home to the world's fastest one-mile dirt track.

Tractor pulls, along with truck pulling, have become serious competition since the first tractor pull in 1929. This truck driver makes a full pull at the 1986 Illinois State Fair Truck and Tractor Pull.

One of the oldest events at the fair, harness racing expanded rapidly in the 1960s and continues to attract large crowds of spectators.

*P*resident Dwight Eisenhower made an official visit in 1954 for Governor's Day activities. Eisenhower poses with Bonigail Bivin and her grand champion steer. Governor William Stratton is to the left of Eisenhower.

*K*ettle corn made in the Conservation World area is a popular treat with spectators watching the lumberjack or raptor shows.

A contestant slips and falls during a log rolling contest at the lumberjack show held in the Conversation World.

*F*ifty drill teams and drum and bugle corps from all over the state competed at the 1957 fair. The Alamo Rangers Junior Drum Corps performs in front of a capacity crowd.

A very tall Uncle Sam makes his way from the main gate during the fair parade.

A procession of people representing various clubs and organizations walk up the hill from the main gate during the 1955 fair. During the 1950s there were daily parades from the main gate. The new Illinois Building gleams in the background.

This little fellow needed a nap break from the excitement at a state fair.

Baby competitions have been a popular attraction at the fair for over a hundred years. Infants have been judged on size, looks, health and, in more recent times, speed. Contestants in the Diaper Derby are readied for the race.

Children's activities have long been a part of the fair. Children's Day often opened the fair. One of the competitions associated with children's day was the Ponytail/Pigtail contest seen here.

Diana Stratton, daughter of Governor and Mrs. William G. Stratton, crowns the Junior King and Queen of the 1957 Illinois State Fair, Steven Squires and Janet Miller.

Winners in the 1954 Illinois State Fair baton twirling contest pose with their trophies. From left are Bonita Rae Stanek, Susan Keith and Robert Funk.

This cheerleading squad from Momence, Illinois gives its all during the cheer-leading competition at the state fair which has been held since 1980.

*G*arbed in a stereotypical farmer's outfit, this man shows his technique during the Hog Calling contest.

*T*he Auctioneer's Bid Calling Contest draws many participants from around the state, waiting to put their skills to the test to see who becomes Grand Champion. Lance Schmid of Clinton, Illinois was the 1991 state fair champion.

HOW TO CALL A HUSBAND

*A*big mouth aided by imaginative props and costumes helps determine the winners in the Husband Calling competition at the fair—a take off on the popular hog calling contests.

*D*ecked out in garters, derby hat and fake mustache, Edward Kaizer of Peoria plays his way to first place in the 1986 Illinois State Fair's Olde Tyme Piano Playing Contest.

*T*he Illinois Pork Cookoff has been a fair staple since the mid-1960s. This concentrating chef prepares to serve his pork ribs.

*M*rs. Beverly Sheehan and Mrs. Josephine Dayton place finishing touches on "the ultra-modern in formal table settings" according to a press release of about 1950.

The installation of a large refrigeration unit in the Dairy Building made it possible for an Illinois State Fair butter cow. In 1922, J.D. Wallace became its first sculptor. The sculpture has become somewhat of a folk tradition for fairgoers. Made over a wood and wire frame with close to 500 pounds of unsalted butter (salt would draw out moisture) the cow varies, but is always a dairy cow. Sometimes it has the addition of a calf or milkmaid, dog or cat.

In recent years two people in particular are remembered for their creative talents with butter while working two to three days in temperature near 38°F. Frank Dutt sculpted the cow for over ten years before Norma "Duffy" Lyon took over. Lyon's work has attracted visitors for over 30 years, completing her last cow in 2001 before retiring.

Fair Today, Fair Tomorrow

The Illinois State Fair has adapted to a century-and-one-half of changing social, cultural, economic and, most importantly, agricultural developments. By constantly meeting new challenges and conditions and redefining its role and image, the fair has not only survived, but remained a thriving, vital Illinois event. Today's fair means tradition—farm machinery, contests, parades, horse shows and a midway. But it also means cutting-edge technology, Ethnic Village, Home and Garden workshops and high dive thrills. The sights, sounds and smells of the fair are many and familiar. They range from the warm, earthy smell of tack and horse barns and the aroma of French fries, elephant ears and corn dogs frying, to the ear-piercing scream of tires and roaring engines at the auto races and the laughter of baby races. The fair has a rich her-

Typical state fair weather—hot and humid—dictates cool clothing. Ballcaps, shorts, t-shirts and comfortable shoes are familiar dress for the Illinois State Fair.

itage but is also a celebration of today and tomorrow. Change and tradition go hand in hand at the Illinois State Fair.

For so many Illinois people the fair is the biggest and best party of the summer. Husband or hog-calling, Decorated Diaper contests and children's games from the 1800s can be found around the corner from Main Street USA or an Elvis impersonator belting out Jailhouse Rock. 4-H exhibits, master gardener demonstrations, face painting, crafts, computer labs, Sand Castle, orange Dreamsicles and sideshow barkers all mix in the world that assembles for over a week every August then disappears in a flash.

A stroll through today's fair is amusing, educating, edifying, and exciting. All in all, from the Giant Slide to the closing fireworks, the state fair is a celebration in the best sense of the word.

*L*ivestock judging competitions remain an important aspect of the state fair. Here mule draft teams are judged in the coliseum, swine in the Junior Livestock Barn and a boy receives an award in the Sheep Barn. Presenting the award is Joe Hampton, director of the Illinois Department of Agriculture.

*S*ince 1902 the Coliseum building has served as the main stage for livestock shows at the state fair.

*T*he state fair has promoted agriculture for 150 years—in farm equipment displays, livestock competitions and agricultural product exhibits.

Songs, dances and other performances representing various cultures and exotic food offerings make the Ethnic Village a popular site for fairgoers seeking food, relaxation and entertainment.

*T*he fastest harness racing track in North America, with a speed rating today of 2.01, premiered at the 1894 State Fair, and has been a permanent part of the Grand Circuit since 1930.

*T*he U.S.A.C. car races at the State Fair feature both the Tony Bettenhausen Memorial 100 Mile Dirt Car Championship and the Allen Crowe Memorial Late Model Stack Car Championship.

*F*rom the early '20s until 1967 the last day of the fair was traditionally motorcycle race day. Unfortunately a small group of peace-disturbing fans ended the races during fair week.

*T*he Midway attracts both young and old, offering games, rides, sideshows and prizes such as the traditional test of strength of ringing the bell.

*B*right, colorful lights on carnival rides add an extra spectrum to the Midway after night falls on the Illinois State Fair.

The wide choice of food at the state fair makes for tough decisions. These people stand in front of but a small selection of food stands located at the fair.

Since its opening in 1894 the Exposition Building has been home to commercial exhibitors who entice crowds with everything from vacuum sweepers and musical instruments to kitchen gadgets and health care products.

Farmers, gardeners and fruit growers have brought their produce to the fair for competition since the first fair in 1853.

The fair's adaptability in meeting new interests is shown in Tech Town while retaining its traditional educational and entertaining agricultural exhibits.

*T*he giant yellow slide has provided no frills thrills at the fair since 1968.

*F*or a different view of the fair visitors enjoy the Skyride traveling from the milkshake stand near the Grandstand to Ethnic Village and beyond.

*S*tate Fair weather isn't always fair, but these folks won't let a little rain spoil their enjoyment of the Twilight Parade as it heads north on Ninth Street.

*F*ddle contestants young and old bring melodic folk ballads and feet stomping dance music to the stage.

*A*ll it takes is a big smile with a well cared for set of teeth to enter the annual Illinois Dental Association sponsored Smile Contest.

A good game of horseshoes becomes intense when a State Fair tournament championship is involved.

*B*eginning shortly after the Civil War the State Fair has honored veterans with programs and free admission on Veterans' Day.

*K*iddie Land, later called Adventure Village, provides rides for the young.

*A*t the Lincoln Stage amateur and professional talent offers something every day for all ages to enjoy.

*O*ver one million visitors attend the Illinois State Fair each year. Illinois flags line the drive outside the Exposition Building in this photo.

*F*ree entertainment is provided all over the fairgrounds. This boy takes a shot at a basket held by very tall Gator the Clown.

*S*ome parents prefer strollers while others choose backpacks but either method makes a useful way to transport children across the vast fairground acreage.

*M*any fairgoers don't consider their fair visit complete without a Grandstand Show, whether it is a return of favorites such as Alabama, Willie Nelson or the Beach Boys (above left) or the latest pop stars.

*T*he fair officially opens with a ribbon cutting ceremony. Here the 2001 Miss Illinois County Fair Queen, Jenn Scheitlin offers an opening welcome.

*F*reworks after each night's Grandstand shows draws a fun filled day at the fair to a close.

ACKNOWLEDGEMENTS

We are sincerely grateful to the numerous individuals who contributed their assistance to the creation of this book. In the Illinois Department of Agriculture, Harold "Bud" Ford, Illinois State Fair Manager, opened the historical records of the fair for our use. His staff, including Abbe Eldred, Dennis Morris and Penney Welch, generously donated their time and knowledge to help us through difficult questions. The help of John Herath, Chief Public Information Officer, was invaluable in navigating the produc-

tion from idea to completion. At the Illinois State Historical Library, Director Kathryn Harris and photograph librarian Mary Michaels were resourceful and diligent in locating and reproducing historical photographs. And finally, as always, we are thankful for the great pleasure of working with publisher Brad Baraks.

The Authors

AUTHORS

Edward J. Russo

Edward J. Russo is Springfield's City Historian and author of *Prairie of Promise, a History of Springfield and Sangamon County*, and co-author of *Greater Springfield, Building of the Legacy*. He is a native of Springfield and has had a life-long interest in local history, has taught architectural history courses, and serves as a Springfield Historic Sites' Commissioner. In addition, Russo has written dozens of articles on Springfield history.

Melinda Garvert

A native of Springfield, Melinda Garvert received her bachelor's and master's degrees from Illinois State University. She began her career as an elementary teacher, later taught at I.S.U., and worked as a school librarian. In 1985 she joined the staff of Lincoln Library's Sangamon Valley Collection. Garvert has worked as a volunteer at the Illinois State Museum and is active in the Sangamon County Historical Society, as well as the Elijah Iles House Foundation.

Curtis Mann

Curtis Mann is a librarian with the Sangamon Valley Collection at Lincoln Library in Springfield. Originally from southern Illinois, he received his bachelor's degree in history from Southern Illinois University and his master's degree in Library Science from the University of Illinois. Mann currently serves as secretary for the Sangamon County Historical Society. He has co-authored with Russo and Garvert a four-part pictorial history on Springfield: *Springfield Business, Springfield Entertainment, Springfield Home and Family,* and *Springfield Community Service.*

State Building, State Fair Grounds, Springfield, Ill.

Snap Shot in State Fair Grounds, Springfield, Ill.

Dairy Building, State Fair Grounds, Springfield, Ill.

THIS BUNGALOW BUILT OF LUMBER, MILL WORK AND OTHER MATERIALS SOLD BY SEARS, ROEBUCK AND CO. CHICAGO, ILL.

SEARS, ROEBUCK AND CO.'S AGRICULTURAL EXHIBIT AND REST BUNGALOW FOR FREE USE OF VISITORS AT SPRINGFIELD STATE FAIR.